A VISION OF THE WAY THE CELTIC CHURCH GREW IN IRELAND, PICTLAND, WALES, BRITAIN

600 B.C. TO 600 A.D.

Brother Ronald S.S.F.
(Society of St Francis)

Pen and ink drawings
by
Jane Pape

Campaign Literature
Saltcoats

Published in Great Britain by
Campaign Literature

First Edition 2000

I.S.B.N. 1 872463 17 7

Printed in Great Britain by
Campaign Literature
Adelaide College
Nineyard Street
Saltcoats
Ayrshire KA21 5HS

A Vision of the way the Celtic Church grew in Ireland, Pictland, Wales, Britain

600 B.C. to 600 A.D.

Appreciations

It is rather refreshing that Brother Ronald, an Anglican Franciscan Friar, has taken a genuine interest in the early "Celtic Church". During his travels he has observed and noted several important issues which he raises in his publication, two very meaningful points being:

> (i)   his confirmed belief, which I share, that Christianity had arrived in Britain at a very early period.

> (ii)   "Why is our earliest Church hidden?".

Why, indeed? This is a cry from the heart in the form of a fundamental inquiry; not a challenge, but an appeal to scholars to carry out a thorough and unbiased research on a subject that has been curbed and even misrepresented ever since the Roman Legions invaded Britain. Brother Ronald highlights our heritage and culture in a caring manner, which will interest both scholar and casual reader alike.

Edward Peterson, F.S.A. (Scot.)

This useful guide for historian and novice alike combines Brother Ronald's research and many miles of trekking in order to meet with and talk to the archaeologist and historian alike. I met him at the Whithorn Dig and the Botel Bailey Excavation. He has visited both sites and many others during his journeys through the Highlands and Islands and down the western coasts of our Celtic lands.   His enthusiasm, like his faith, has never, nor will ever, wane.   His ideas and his research have contributed greatly to our current understanding of the history of the early Celtic Church.

> *Alastair Penman*
> Field Archaeologist, in the year 2000 A.D.

This vision of the "Celtic Church" described by an Anglican Franciscan Friar combines an account of a journey on foot in the Scottish Highlands with a meditation on the presence of God in the countryside. The growth of the Christian church in the early Middle Ages in Britain and Ireland, starting at Candida Casa (Whithorn) and moving later to Iona, is feelingly told.

The writer's declared purpose in travelling was to meet with other "intercessors" – people who like himself, believe in the power of prayer. His particular preoccupation is with Celtic Christianity, which he perceives as distinct in kind from that of the later medieval church, with a special holiness of its own.

Many readers will share these enthusiasms, and will enjoy the simplicity and imagination with which this little book is written.

Daphne Brooke
Historian and Lecturer
for the Adult Education Department
of Glasgow University, March 2000.

Acknowledgements

I am deeply indebted to Ernestine Roach for her encouragement, patience, and painstaking efforts to type from innumerable pages of handwritten notes.

Also to Miss Angela Butler for introducing me to the people of the Outer Hebridean Islands of Harris and Lewis, for introducing me to the artist Jane Pape, and for her grammatical text advice.

Illustrations were essential for this book and I am profoundly thankful to Jane Pape for her great patience and sensitivity, both spiritual and practical, producing exactly what was needed.

I also want to thank those who helped me when I first struggled to express on paper what I was discovering.

I am also grateful for the help given by librarians of the Iona Community at the Abbey, and the Northumbria Community at Nether Springs, Hetton Hall.

My thanks also to the 'Come Back to God' Campaign Team and Adelaide College, not only for caring for my bodily needs, but also for offering to publish this book.

*Dun Carloway Pictish Broch on the Isle of Lewis
(see Chapter 2)*

Contents

Between 600 B.C. and 600 A.D.

A Traveller's Vision

of

How God Prepared For The

Planting

And Then Tended

The Growth Of His Church

In These Islands

By 'these islands' I mean all that can be found, large or small, in the area covered by the sketch map on the next page, remembering that Pictland is now Scotland.

During the course of travels in these islands over many years I chanced to meet archaeologists and historians and gathered information which I saved and pieced together until I began to get a vision of the earliest Church which, for many reasons, has been hidden from us.

This map is to help the reader to quickly identify places mentioned in the B.C.period

SHETLAND IS.

ORKNEY IS.

IS. OF LEWIS

HEBRIDEAN ISLANDS

HARRIS

INVERNESS

PICTLAND (PICTS)

IS. OF SKYE

IS. OF IONA

IS. OF LISMORE

HOLY ISLAND LINDISFARNE

DALRIADA SCOTS IN PICTLAND

GALLOWAY

NORTHUMBRIA

DALRIADA (SCOTS)

SOLWAY FIRTH

WHITHORN

(PICTS)

IS.OF MAN (MANX)

BRITAIN (BRITONS) (ANGLES) (SAXONS)

IRELAND

WALES

CORNWALL

BRITTANY

GAUL

Chapter 1

A Traveller's Discoveries
And Vision

Let us begin by considering how travellers make discoveries. Take, for example, a group of fell walkers who are sensitive to the beauty of God's creation, setting out on a good summer's day with all five senses alert, sight, hearing, smell, touch and taste. They will quickly find edible berries and will be picking up the scent of wild flowers and herbs, hearing the sound of a grasshopper and exploring for a few minutes the wonders of the insect world. The sound of bubbling water draws them to a spring where they are refreshed by the purity of the water. A birdsong may attract their attention and they witnessthe courtship of species they have never seen before.

Then, reaching the top of a hill, they are silenced by a view that is breathtaking, a galaxy of colours, bright clouds in a blue sky, a landscape patterned with sunshine and shadows, an expanse of sparkling water with islands on the horizon.

Another discovery is the experience of walking through the heather in the Highlands, finding a majestic thistle, and seeing the beauty and grandeur of rock formations. All this, and so much more is the work of a master artist, our Creator God.

Let us stay with the travellers for another experience they would never forget. Coming down a mountain, stepping cautiously because of drains hidden in long grass that have broken many legs, they scent the smoke of a peat fire - someone's home. Then, meeting a shepherd, they hear a tale of his or her ancestors, and they would realise that beneath their feet was evidence of a very early community, many centuries B.C.

This is exactly how my personal trail of discovery began, many years ago.

The Spirit of God and a Shepherd's Faith

I was living for two weeks with a shepherd and his wife in a very remote Scottish valley. Their nearest neighbour was another shepherd who was four miles down the valley, a treacherous bog between them, and no path, not even a sheep track. The only tree to be seen was a small rowan close to the shepherd's cottage. Among the hills there were rocky outcrops, colourful in the sunlight but ominous and forbidding under darkening clouds, and the whole valley with its pools, streams and grasses reflected the beauty and wonder of creation. There was a mysterious beauty about that place though it was fraught with many dangers.

Bill and Mair had never travelled anywhere; shepherding was their whole life. Their faith was simple, and very real. They knew God in a personal way and trusted Him. Bill went out with his two dogs to round up the sheep in violent storms and appalling weather conditions. Blizzards completely isolated them for weeks. He said he was never afraid, because the Lord was with him. He could say with David the Shepherd Psalmist "Though I walk through the valley of the shadow of death I fear no evil. Thou art with me." (Psalm 23).

We talked about the prophecy in Joel 2 v 28, when God said "I will pour out My Spirit on all flesh"; Then how Jesus promised the gift of His Holy Spirit to teach, strengthen and enable us to do His will, and how at the very moment of our talking about these promises we were in fact experiencing the fellowship of the Holy Spirit. As we looked down the valley the opening words of the Bible came to mind, 'The Spirit of God was brooding over the face of the waters'.

Gathering Fragments of Precious Information

The purpose of all my travelling was entirely for meeting intercessors who believed in the power of intercessory prayer, and the reality of spiritual warfare, and who were praying for our chronically sick world, both as individuals and in small groups. I was especially anxious to meet those in prayer support networks for world evangelistic and relief organisations who were responding to the desperate cries for help coming from the victims of savage tribal wars, natural disasters, and the appalling slavery and abuse of millions of children. Among all these pleadings to God for help, prayer for Israel is high on the agenda. Many have gone out to give aid and share the love of God with the teaching of Jesus. They need networks of intercessors and prayer supporters.

The meetings with archaeologists and historians were, at first, incidental but became increasingly important. They began in South

The shepherd with his mule, laden with grain, ready for the six mile trek across boggy ground and over a steep hill to his cottage.

West Scotland at Whithorn, then on the Isle of Iona and the Outer Hebridean Islands of Lewis and Harris.

The gathering of information was rather like accidentally finding pieces of a very large jigsaw puzzle, saving them until pieces from different parts of the puzzle began to fit together and gradually beginning to see what the picture was all about.   Hopefully the linking up chronologically of the information I have collected will give the reader a picture or vision of the hidden Christian Church in these islands during the first six hundred years of the first millennium A.D.

Why is our Earliest Church Hidden?

Most of us have to say that neither our history books nor our school teachers gave us knowledge of its existence.   It was not even mentioned in most churches.   We were told about a monk called Columba, who, together with twelve friends who were monks, sailed in a coracle from Ireland and landed on the Isle of Iona.   We thought that was a foolish thing to do!   There was also a Roman soldier named Alban who was killed because he was a Christian. In Ireland some stories about early saints were told.   Why is it that so many churches throughout the islands are named after saints, and the people who go to these churches know very little or nothing about the patron saint?

Most people still think that the Christian Church was not established here until after Augustine landed on the Isle of Thanet in 597 A.D., incidentally, that same year in which St.Columba died on the Isle of Iona.

The truth about the earliest Church in these islands has been hidden from us because written evidence has been destroyed or buried, and because chroniclers and then historians wrote with both a political and a denominational bias, thus creating a chain of error through the centuries to this present day.

With the new technology for dating artefacts and a desire to present the truth, archaeologists and historians are working closely together re-examining the earliest stones and manuscripts, while reports of new discoveries frequently hit the headlines.

Chapter 2

The Earliest People On
These Islands

Hopefully, these pages will stimulate interest and encourage readers to make their own investigations. With this in mind certain places, people and events have been given more attention, even to some detail, because they help to clarify the vision that is being shared.

At the beginning of the period we are considering, from 600 B.C. onwards, Palestine was well into the Iron Age. Nebuchadnezzar, King of Babylon, destroyed Jerusalem and deported the Children of Israel to Babylon in captivity. See the Book of Daniel.

Here in these islands the Iron Age was just emerging from the Bronze Age. There is ample evidence of the Stone Age inhabitants and by the time of the Bronze Age, hunters, farmers, fishermen and sea traders were well established. A strong Pictish Kingdom was emerging. Pictland did not become Scotland until A.D. 843, when Kenneth MacAlpin, King of the Scots in Dal Riada, by clever scheming became High King of the Picts.

The Gaelic-speaking Scots were first based in the extreme north of Ireland, called Dal Riada, with recurrent suggestions in Irish mythology that they came from Spain. The names Scot, Gael, and Dal Riada can be traced to names in fragments of early chronicles and genealogies that go right back to the story of Creation and Noah.

The Picts were also strong in Ireland, mainly in the region of Bangor. People outside Ireland today often forget the Irish Picts because so much publicity has been given to Pictish stone memorials in Scotland.

How did the Picts get their name?   It is strange that we have no record of the name Pict or Picti until A.D.297 when it appeared in a Latin poem.   The name means 'painted' and was used by Roman soldiers to describe them.   The Picts were seen tattooed and painted with woad.   This would have been helpful to them for purposes of identification as tribe members in the forest-covered mountains, and as camouflage in guerilla warfare.   The nickname given by the Roman soldiers was embellished later to give the impression that Picts were wild savages, and this was done by both Romans and Scots for political purposes.

Everywhere in these islands sovereign kingdoms were emerging, the Manx in the Isle of Man, Cornish in Cornwall, Bretons in Brittany, several among the Welsh in Wales and among the Britons in Britain where also there was an influx of Angles and Saxons. The Kings of Pictland and of the surrounding islands were all subservient to the High King of the Picts at Inverness.

From the very earliest times tribal warfare and slave raids called for constant preparation for both attack and defence.   Small kingdoms were established and often quickly overthrown.   Stone brochs and fortresses were essential.

The indigenous people were experienced in the use of stone.   The masonry and positioning of brochs on steep slopes are reminders of the skills of early Armenian architects and builders.   They withstood not only the assaults in many tribal battles but also the torrential rain and gales of hundreds of years.

The Dun Carloway Broch (see frontispiece) has outside walls sloping inwards with inner walls that are vertical. Between them are galleries linked and bonded together by stone slabs which form the steps. The largest chambers are on the ground floor.

Among all the above mentioned people were Celts, who for centuries had come as sea traders, settled and penetrated these islands, and as a result of their influence there were later references to Picti Celts and Scotti Celts.   People who talk about the Celtic Church in Scotland often completely overlook the fact that for four or five hundred years, it was as much the Pictish Church as it was the Celtic Church.

*The Pictish Broch at Glen Elg in the North
Western Highlands.*

Chapter 3

By 600 B.C. Merchant Ships From Norway And The Mediterranean Had Created Important Lines Of Communication

By 600 B.C. the main roads of the world were sea roads and the secondary roads were the rivers. About that time the Prophet Jonah tried to escape from doing God's will and going to Nineveh. He boarded a ship going to Tarshish in Spain which was regarded as the edge of the world. Archaeological evidence today shows Tarshish to be near Seville.

Phoenician biremes, with two banks of oars, were regularly taking merchants to Tarshish and from there smaller vessels went from port to port up to the Scilly Isles.

In these islands the hunters were still busy, but more were involved in animal husbandry and farming, living in small communities. They were great days of barter, when merchants gathered in noisy market places before the Celts introduced coins. Merchant ships came from Norway, Gaul and Mediterranean countries for gold, silver, copper, tin, lead, leather and wool. From Norway came furs, walrus ivory and amber. From Gaul and the Mediterranean came pottery, glassware, oil, wine, and metal products for farming and warfare. Archaeologists have found such a harvest of artefacts on the Solway coast that it may well have been the centre of international trading in these islands.

A glance at the sketch map *(see Page 2)* will show its centrality. The Norse traders came from the Orkneys via the Hebridean Islands to Argyll and Galloway; the Mediterranean traders via Spain, Iberia, Brittany, Cornwall, Wales, Ireland and into the Solway.

With the development of international sea-trading the buying and selling of slaves became more profitable, not just for their physical labour but for their many skills and languages. Planning some of these journeys must have been very difficult without maps. It was not until the second century A.D. that Ptolemy, the Alexandrian geographer, produced a map *(see Page 13)* that was still in use when the Venerable Bede was writing, but Pictland was so misshapen that it was the cause of false information being given about the movements of Picts and Scots.

Edward Peterson describes this clearly in his book 'The Message of Scotland's Symbol Stones.'

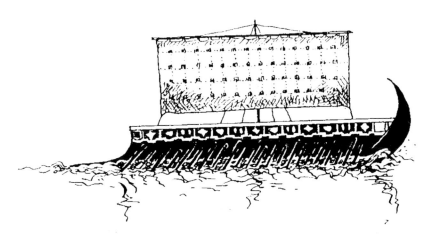

A Phoenician bireme. Vessels like this travelled from the Eastern Mediterranean to Tarshish in Spain.

1800 year old Roman boat found by archaeologists at Newport in Gwent, showing earlier Celtic shipbuilding technology.
The constructed model is in Newport Museum, giving a good idea of its appearance.

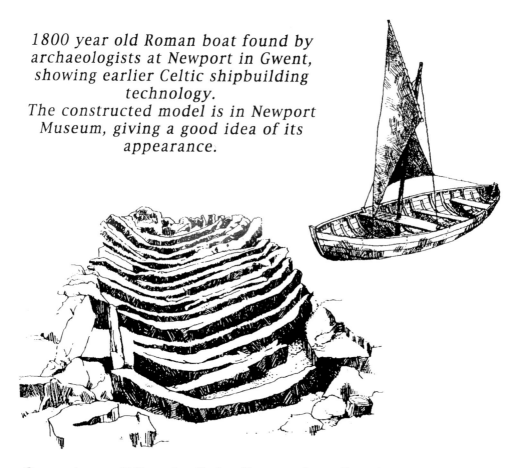

Coracles, Hide-hulled Curraghs & Merchant Ships

Before the Romans built roads the rivers were their roads, and it is well worth looking at a map of Scotland and tracing rivers to their sources. Traders and armed forces travelled to a river source, then with the help of horses kept there they moved to the next river source and continued their journey. This is why the Picts had such a great advantage over the Roman legions in guerrilla warfare.

Much publicity has been given to coracles, even the small ones that children can control, because of St.Columba's, and also St.Brendan's voyage from Western Ireland in a hide-hulled curragh. This has meant that many people are unaware of the skills of these islanders in shipbuilding with well seasoned timber.

Archaeologists have recently found a third century A.D. Roman boat very well constructed of oak, and thirty eight feet long, preserved under five feet of mud near Newport in Gwent. It was capable of carrying about three tons of cargo, and probably used fore and aft sails. It is worth noting that archaeologists said it was built to an earlier Celtic design that had been lost.

Chapter 4

The Celts Advanced Westwards

Who Were the Celts?

Under both fact and fiction so many stories have been written about the Celts that people believe what they want to believe about them. Historians themselves continue to disagree over dates, names and places. I can only share what I have found that relates to my vision of the growth of the early Church.

The Celts originally came from Southern Russia, near the Caspian Sea. They were farmers and salt miners who traded with the Greeks and Romans. Diodorus, the Greek historian of the first century B.C., described them as having a terrifying appearance, tall, with bleached hair, thick and shaggy like a horse's mane, with brightly coloured cloaks fastened with a brooch. In 33 B.C. Alexander the Great described them as tall, bearded, with long hair, carrying long lances and small round shields. It is recorded somewhere that they had their horses bridled for many centuries B.C. Clearly the Greeks and the Romans were afraid of them. The Celts sacked Rome in 390 B.C. and were at war with Rome on three occasions after that.

The Celts could never be described as a nation because they lived in several distinct tribal groupings, each with its own warlord. It is therefore remarkable that they had a common language, gods and goddesses, and very interesting characteristics, such as their love of colour, skills in design, and a very strong commitment to helping the poor, the sick, and the elderly.

As they advanced westwards along the Danube they overcame the Etruscans, already famous for their metalwork. The Celts added their skills in ironwork for farm implements, weapons, swords and knives, and became more involved in sea-trading, using the routes that brought them to the islands around Britain.   They crossed the Rhine, conquered Gaul and Northern Spain.

The Celts Arrive in these Islands

They never conquered Britain as the Romans did, but penetrated as traders meeting traders, farmers meeting farmers, establishing relationships over a very long period.   They had so much to share. There could have been many skirmishes as tribal feuds were common.   There is no record of ferocious cavalry charges as in earlier conquests.   They penetrated these islands by a gradual infiltration.   The combined skills in warfare of Britons and Celts enabled the Britons to prevent the two invasion attempts by Julius Caesar in B.C.55 and 53.

Celtic Influence on Indigenous Languages

The Celts had no writing until the Fifth Century A.D. and so depended upon an oral tradition.   They were reputed to be great storytellers.   The telling or singing of heroic adventures and encounters in battle seems to have been the order of the day! Although they had a common language the different tribal groupings also developed their own language.

The Goedelic-speaking Celts were responsible for the Irish Gaelic language spoken by the Scots in Dal-Riada, the Manx of the Isle of Man, and later by highlanders and people of the Western Islands.

The Brythonic-speaking Celts had the frequent use of 'p' in their language, and that could be found in Brittany, Cornwall, Wales, and among the Picts.   This was a great help for people travelling between Pictland and Brittany, and accounted for some close family relationships between Pictland, North Britain and Wales.

As we are looking at God's timing and see how the sea trade routes were being prepared for carrying the Gospel, the Celts' language links made it easier for people in these islands to communicate with Gaul and the rest of Europe.

Gods and Goddesses and Spiritual Warfare

The early Celts were farmers and fishermen with a religion that had close connections with the forces of nature and the environment, and so had many gods and goddesses. The most important were Epona the Horse Goddess, Elen the Water Goddess, and the Earth Mother. Votive offerings were usually gifts of flowers, pieces of clothing and small images of their family gods. When the Celts had enjoyed the adventure of a battle and returned home with the heads of enemy chiefs on the points of their lances, they embalmed and hung some of them in their shrines. They were in spiritual bondage to their gods and goddesses, to serve them in this way.

Occasionally, to appease the anger of the gods, human sacrifices were necessary and there were times when men and women offered themselves to die for their tribe. The Celts found the Picts and Irish serving similar gods and goddesses, and this would have helped integration. With ample archaeological evidence it is easier for us now to list the gods of the Picts and Irish. Foremost were the sun, moon, stars and Mother Earth, rocks, water, and fire, altogether requiring four major seasonal sacrifices.

Mother goddesses in Ireland like Sheela and Bridget (Bride) controlled fertility and protected the tribes. In South West Pictland the missionaries of St.Ninian from Whithorn encountered the worship of the goddess Medan. The Celts believed in reincarnation that could happen many times and take many forms.

These creatures were worshipped: the whale and seal, lion, bear, bull, boar, fox and the snake. The Celts were very conscious of the spirit of good and evil in the spirit world. Earthly warfare and spiritual warfare were intertwined. It is amazing how many birds they also worshipped, especially birds associated with war, like the raven, the crane, and the goose. The Irish war-raven goddess in sculpture was shown with a cluster of human heads surrounded by birds of war. The Picts and the Norsemen had the goose as a symbol of war because it was fierce and aggressive to other birds as well as to human beings.

It is significant that the Celts lived much more in fear of their gods and goddesses than in fear of any human enemy. The spirit world of good and evil was as real to them as the material world.

Today, here in the West, people are hardly aware that they are human beings with spirits who have been given bodies and souls. The material world is the only reality for them.

Druids - the Wise Men of the Celts

There can be no mention of the Celts without Druids coming into people's minds, and again the blending of fact and fiction has been a cause of widespread misunderstanding.

There is a tendency to think of Druids only as priests responsible for religious rites and ceremonies. Some were priests, but Druids were statesmen and judges, responsible for the judicial system and education, and among them were poets, musicians and bards too. It took twenty years of intensive learning to qualify as a Druid.

Laertius, the 3rd Century AD Greek author, wrote that the Druids were men of culture, equitable and impartial in the administration of justice. They instituted colleges of physicians. They were described as expecting every member of the tribe to reverence the deity, to abstain from evil, and to behave valiantly.

Among the Druids were ascetics, searching for the truth, recognised as holy men, and living under stringent self-discipline. They believed in a life after death and aspired to qualify for a high-ranking place among the ruling gods of Elysium. They had heard of Zeus sending Apollo to earth, and that he was a valiant man who died, returned to Zeus, and then came back to earth again.

By the time the emperor Julius Caesar attempted to invade Britain, the Druids were already teaching Latin and Greek, and that was ninety years before the conquest of Britain. Because Jews would have been in the trade ships from the Mediterranean as merchants or slaves, some of the Druids would have been aware of the Torah and the Messianic prophesies.

Chapter 5

An Awesome Act Of God

God Sending His Son to Save the World

"God so loved the world that He gave His only begotten Son, that whoever believes in Him should not perish but have everlasting life!" (Gospel of St.John, Chapter 3 verse 16)

A young Jewish virgin gave birth to a boy, as the Angel Gabriel had foretold and as prophesied hundreds of years before. As instructed by the Angel He was named Jesus, because He would deliver His people from their sins. The experience of the shepherds at Bethlehem would have been the first item of news to be spread around. The most sensational story would have been King Herod's slaughter of small boys in Bethlehem. That came about because of the visit of the three Wise Men from the East, guided by a star, bringing gifts of gold, frankincense and myrrh for the child they believed to be a Divinely appointed King. This item of news from Palestine would soon have been carried on the tradeships going west. The teaching of Jesus, His miracles of healing, and raising the dead were the next sensational items of news to be carried abroad, only to be followed by news of His crucifixion and resurrection from the dead.

An interesting legend in Ireland tells of how Conor MacNessar, the King of Ulster who died in A.D.48, knew about the happenings in Palestine at the time of the Crucifixion, and asked his chief Druid, Bacrach, for an explanation of the great darkness that was over all the earth.

Then followed the most sensational news to be carried abroad, Jesus' Ascension into Heaven and the outpouring of the Holy Spirit at

Pentecost. The Apostles preached in Jerusalem, using the languages of different nations represented there, and called for repentance, explaining the forgiveness of sins and the offer of the gift of the Holy Spirit; all because of the perfect offering of Jesus, the sinless One, upon the Cross.

Miracles of healing followed the preaching of the Good News. That was when the floodgates of gossip were opened and the world was to hear all about it. Eyewitnesses and some who had been miraculously healed could soon have been on the merchant ships. The ascetics and holy ones among the Druids on these islands would have taken these stories from Palestine seriously and been eagerly waiting to meet an eyewitness, and these could have been among the merchants themselves, including Messianic Jews, the first to recognise that Jesus was truly their Messiah.

Also the slave trade was booming and one wonders how many of the earliest Christian slaves found their way into the households of Druids. Some slaves were more fortunate than others, being wanted for their skills and language and not just for hard labour. The period we are considering was the middle of the great Han Dynasty in China and they had opened the Silk Road to trade with the Roman Empire. Slaves were transported on this route and there is a record of slaves from Ireland being taken to the East.

The persecution of Christians had begun by Jews and by Romans. Christian merchants in Palestine, aware of Jesus' prophesying the Fall of Jerusalem and foreseeing this event, which happened in A.D.70, could well have taken their families away by boats, using the trade routes to get as far away as possible from Roman domination.

Among historians and archaeologists there are many who are convinced that by the time of the Roman conquest of Britain small groups of Christians were active in these islands, some more hidden than others, in an otherwise totally pagan society. Seeds of the Gospel were sown! The Glastonbury legends of Jesus being brought as a child and the visit of Joseph of Arimathaea are not to be ignored. There are so many legends that may have been distorted through the centuries, but as the earliest records are re-examined the truth that is hidden in them will be revealed.

An early chronicler wrote that certain friends and disciples of our Lord found refuge in Britain in A.D.37 in the persecution that followed His ascension. Another chronicler mentioned Judean refugees in these islands.

Chapter 6

What Was Happening In Pictland, Ireland And The Hebridean Islands

From Dal-Riada in Northern Ireland the Gaelic-speaking Scots had penetrated Pictland and established bases in the Central Argyll area. They launched attacks on the Picts but were always defeated during the six hundred years we are reviewing, but were able to stay under Pictish rule.   It is interesting that the Irish Picts and Irish Scots managed to live fairly close to one another.   There were skirmishes but probably trading and the need of mutual support against any attacks by other enemies helped to keep the peace.   Also there were Christians among the Scots and the Picts which made it easier for the earliest missionaries to travel about Ireland.

The stronghold of the Pictish people was in the Highlands and the east side of Pictland.   The Picts with their Norse and Celtic blood were ready to take on any foe, and this the Romans were about to discover.   To die in battle was the greatest honour for the Pict, as it was for the Norseman.

Standing Stones, Symbol Stones, and Brochs

Because of insecurity there was no attempt to build permanent homes, although they were capable of using the skills they learned in the Stone Age thousands of years earlier.   They showed remarkable skills with stone in building fortifications, especially brochs which were circular towers, roomy and as strong today as when they were built.   From the very earliest days of the Picts, thousands of years ago, the flora and fauna of the landscape has changed, but the standing stones and symbol stones of the Picts are there to be seen by all of us today.   Some may have been struck by lightning and damaged or fallen, but most are there to tell us the history of these people, their tribal ancestry, and the way they worshipped their gods.   A visit to the Callenish Stones on the Isle of Lewis in the Western Isles will show the latter.

Most of the symbol stones are in the north and east, but symbols of the earliest stones are found in the Western Islands, showing the remarkable communication system in the Pictish Kingdom and the control of the High King of the Picts at Inverness.

The Callenish Stones on the Isle of Lewis
clearly show how the earliest people worshipped the moon.

Through the centuries the symbols increased in number and were wonderfully engraved showing not only tribal information but displaying their many gods and goddesses.   The engraving on some of their memorial stones was the work of artists and dedicated craftsmen using the most intricate of Celtic patterns, even showing people and animals.

Any crosses erected by the earliest Christian families would have been knocked down by hostile neighbours so engravers of memorial stones had to be cautious, and do what the Christians did in Rome. They used symbols, like the fish and the 'Chi-Rho' sign, representing the first two letters of the Greek for Christos.   A very good example of this was found at Kirkmadrine, in the Rhinns of Galloway, Scotland, two memorial stones, each showing a circle divided into four parts, which to the Picts would represent a barrow, or grave with four chambers. For the Christians the 'Chi-Rho' symbol was clear. These were from the end of the fifth century A.D. or early sixth century. They can be seen in the church at Kirkmadrine.

The very early Pictish Symbol Stone at Aberlemno, five miles north of Forfar in Angus.

The Christian Memorial Stone at Kirkmadrine in the Rhinns Of Galloway.

What Happened when Picts and Scots became Christians?

In many village communities their leaders would have been Druids who already knew Latin and Greek, and who, through association with Jewish traders probably knew Hebrew as well. These would have known the Hebrew Scriptures and would have been aware of the Messianic prophesies. They would also have been familiar with the Psalms. The Christians would have met together, some more secretly than others, to Break Bread, sing a hymn, chant Psalms and pray, with teaching from the Druid leader. The secret meetings would have been in districts where other Druids were deep into the occult, in bondage to pagan ritual or just worldly and power seeking.

The gift of the Holy Spirit from Almighty God the Father in Heaven to His adopted children, making them temples of His Holy Spirit, must have been the most exciting and thrilling discovery, reminding the wise Druids of the Pharaoh in Egypt who called together his servants, when Joseph stood before him and said, "Can we find such a one as this, a man in whom is the Spirit of God?" (Genesis 41 v 38).

Add to this their excitement to hear how John the Baptist, when he baptised Jesus, heard God saying "This is my Beloved Son!" and saw the Holy Spirit descend upon Him in the bodily shape of a dove. This was another discovery that God had chosen the dove as His bird symbol of the Holy Spirit. David, the experienced shepherd and Psalmist had cried out "O for the wings of a dove!" He knew that a dove could out fly its predators. It was the dove that brought back the olive leaf to Noah, not the raven. The pagan Celts had been worshipping the raven and aggressive goose, so this was a revelation. The purity of the dove was and is for us today a reminder that the work of the Holy Spirit in us is to make us holy, and so many of the Celtic saints were holy men and women.

There developed a great reverence for the Three Persons in the One God. It was an awesome reverence expressed in the daily singing as they worked at home in the valleys, on the hills and on the sea. They prayed to God and they sang to God. Having worshipped a mother goddess they exhibited a great devotion to Mary, the mother of Jesus.

Because the Celtic tribes depended upon good farming they were used to regular times of the year for their pagan ceremonies, and the Christian calendar reinforced these seasonal times for worship of their Creator God who had redeemed them and was ready to bless them.

There was another dramatic change taking place in the lives of these people. It was in the realm of spiritual warfare. They discovered that the gods they had feared were not gods. Jesus upon the Cross had defeated Satan. This meant an entirely new strategy in spiritual warfare for them. Satan's evil spirits could be cast out, and they could be protected against attacks if they had faith in Jesus.

Chapter 7

The Romans Invade Britain
But Fail To Conquer Pictland

In the minds of the Romans these islands we know as the British Isles were referred to as 'beyond the edge of the world'. Emperor Claudius was determined to conquer them. Julius Caesar tried twice a hundred years earlier but had failed, the indigenous British tribes having been strengthened by the Celts. Claudius already had some useful contacts among British tribes and with clever planning he was ready for the invasion. He sent four well-trained legions from the coast of Gaul under the command of Aulus Plautius. These were followed by all that was needed for the laying of roads, building of forts, villas and residences for Roman officials. Many slaves were brought and these later were sold to wealthy farmers and Druids, who would have been keen to buy slaves who could teach languages.

From what we know of St.Alban we can assume that there could have been secret believers in Jesus among the Roman soldiers. We know that a Centurion with a villa in Gloucester had a Christian wife. The small church close to the Cathedral named St.Mary de Lode was built on the site of this villa. There is a possibility of that Centurion's legion having been the one on duty at the time of the Crucifixion.

Caractacus, whose Celtic name was Caradoc, was a British Tribal King who led the resistance forces. Aulus Plautius defeated him and he was driven into Wales where he again built up resistance forces. Then, after another defeat, he fled to the Northern British tribe Brigantes whose Queen delivered him to the Romans. About that time the Emperor Claudius himself came to Britain. Caractacus and his family were taken as prisoners for a victory parade in Rome.

At a meeting of the Senate Caractacus made a defence speech which won him a standing ovation. The Emperor Claudius released him and gave him a residence which became known as the British Palace. Gladys, the youngest daughter of Caractacus, was a Christian and was renamed Claudia by the Emperor. Caractacus himself became a Christian. Claudia married a Roman Senator who took her back to Britain when he was serving there in the army. The Revd.Dr.Gordon Strachan in a lecture described how St.Paul in his letter to Timothy refers to Pudens, Linus and Claudia. Two of Claudia's daughters, Praxedes and Pudenziana, became saints, and her brother Linus became the second Bishop of Rome.

Whilst the Legions were conquering Britain and having difficulties with Wales, many people with Celtic blood, including Christians, moved northwards and westwards to safer countries. Families lived like gypsies ready to move at any time, because of invaders or tribal warfare which was a common threat.

General Agricola withdraws From Pictland

Between A.D. 80 and 85 General Julius Agricola led the Roman legions into Pictland, which the Romans called Caledonia. His fleet supported him and he penetrated as far as the Grampian hills where, in battle, he soundly defeated the Picts.

A Roman warship c 100 B.C.
The fleet which supported General Agricola as he penetrated Caledonia would undoubtedly have been smaller vessels.

We are told that he was recalled, but it is more than likely he realised the skills of the Picts in guerrilla warfare, combined with their ferocity and speed both on horseback and in boats, up and down rivers and round the coast. The Romans would have been reminded of their countrymen's fears of the early Celts coming into northern Italy and their sudden raids. Agricola went right back to his northern coast of the Solway and from Carlisle to the Tyne, where in 122 A.D. the Emperor Hadrian had to build a wall.

Because the Romans had been trading with the Britons in the ports along the Solway coast the legionnaires probably had a good relationship with the people who were always afraid of sudden Pictish slave raids, Irish too, so the presence of the Roman legions gave them greater security.

It was from the Galloway Hills that Agricola looked at Ireland and considered invading, but was persuaded against this.

Forty years after the emperor Hadrian had built his wall, Antoninus built another wall from the Clyde to the Firth of Forth. Forty years later that was abandoned. Then, in 208 A.D. the Emperor Septimius Severus rebuilt Hadrian's Wall. He died at York, three

A Roman Charioteer

years later. All this showed the strength of the Picts and when the Roman legions left Britain the Picts invaded and almost reached London.

The Romans did not interfere with the Britons' worship of their gods and goddesses provided they recognised the superiority of the Roman sun god. In fact, if they ever had time they might have helped the Britons to build their shrines as they had done for the Celts in Gaul.   Through all these years the underground Christian Church was growing.   Excavations have revealed Roman villas containing Christian Chapels.   A wonderful example is at Lullingstone in Kent where there is also a pagan shrine to a water goddess.

Whilst the Roman legions were still in Britain, something of great importance to the Christian Church was happening in Gaul. A remarkable bishop was there who had an amazing influence in Europe and the islands of Britain, Martin of Tours.

Chapter 8

St. Martin Of Tours -
A.D. 320 — 397

A Founder of the early Celtic
Church

The impact of this great missionary bishop in Gaul is shown by the seven hundred villages in Europe dedicated to him, as well as the great number of Churches there and in the British Isles. We have a full account of him by a contemporary, Sulpicius Severus, a Christian lawyer. Martin was one of the formative characters in European history in the Dark Ages. He was born in Hungary. His father was a high-ranking officer in the Roman army whose promotion necessitated a move to Pavia in North Italy.

At the age of fifteen Martin wanted to become a Christian and be baptised, but he had to wait because parental opposition and the law compelled him to enter into military service. He was an officer in the army for many years. We do not know exactly how many but Christopher Donaldson, author of 'Martin of Tours', is convinced that Martin was in the army for 25 years. His book is important to anyone interested in this vision of the early church.

Striving to live as a Christian in the pagan Roman army, and even longing to become a hermit, often must have caused laughter and ridicule among his fellow officers, especially on the occasion when he cut his officer's cloak in two to cover a naked beggar. But mockery did not deter him, and he was fully accepted among his fellow officers for his care and concern for anyone in need. There was a mutual trust and dependency upon one another in times of siege or battle, and every officer and soldier was so disciplined that every night he must be fully prepared as if there was a battle at daybreak.

Martin was baptised during the time he was in the army, but he was so determined to be a monk, inspired by what he heard about the Desert Fathers in Egypt, that, just when he might have been promoted, he sought to leave the army. When the Emperor Julian heard this he was furious! He accused Martin of cowardice, because a battle was imminent. These were the words of Martin in response: 'If this conduct of mine is ascribed to cowardice and not to faith I will take my stand unarmed before the line of battle tomorrow and, in the Name of the Lord Jesus, protected by the sign of the Cross, and not by shield or helmet, I will safely penetrate the ranks of the enemy.' The next day the enemy sent an embassy of peace and Martin was released.

After leaving the army, Martin continued to experience adventures and challenges to his Christian faith, but it is significant that he put himself under the discipline of St Hilary of Poitiers and then founded a great monastic community at Liguge. This community combined the hermit cell life with corporate worship and going out on missionary journeys to preach the Gospel, heal the sick, and cast out evil spirits.

The early monasteries were more like villages with men and women living in circles of huts, some close to the actual place where they were using their skills, with a central meeting place for corporate worship. Martin's settlement where he trained hermits and missionaries was Marmoutier - 'the place of the big family'.

One day Martin visited a village where there was a pagan temple built by the Romans and beside it a sacred pine tree, both for the worship of Mother Earth and Cybele the Asiatic goddess, greatly venerated by the Romans in festivals at the time of the new moon in March, with a very perverted form of sexual behaviour. This was taking place when Christians were mourning on Good Friday and rejoicing on Easter Day. Martin explained what he was going to do, then with help pulled down the temple. The Celts did not protest because they knew the Romans could build a new one, but they violently protested when he moved to cut down the sacred pine tree.   From its height and age it was probably due for a solemn ritual felling.   It was leaning and they could see which way it would fall; so Martin told them to fell it, and he would stand just where it would fall, saying that God would save him.   As it was crashing down upon him he put out his hand against it, made the sign of the cross, and the tree suddenly swerved round and fell in the opposite direction nearly killing bystanders. Almost everyone then made a profession of faith in the Lord Jesus Christ.

After the death of the Bishop of Tours, the senior bishops of the Church came to appoint a successor. They would already have in mind whom they wanted, but would first formally seek the approval of the Christians in Tours. The people had already made up their minds that they wanted Martin, although he himself had refused

From a basilica in VÉZELAY, St.Martin, making the sign of the cross when the sacred tree was being cut down and would have fallen on him.

to be put forward. So, they tricked him into believing that someone in Tours was very ill and when the crowd had assembled in the square before the appointing bishops, they pushed Martin forward saying they only wanted Martin, and not the men who had been presented to them. The bishops were furious. They said he was unsuitable and unworthy, that he was 'despicable in countenance, his clothing mean, and his hair disgusting!' However, the people shouted until the bishops had to give way.

So, Martin became Bishop of Tours. This did not change his life style but gave him even greater authority as he launched out in evangelism with the skills of a Roman officer, tempered with humility and a great sensitivity to human need. He led his troops of young disciples and subdued the heathen with their evil practices by his sheer holiness of character. Many sick people were healed, evil spirits were cast out and there were reports of the dead being brought back to life.

At the age of eighty, he set off with a band of disciples to settle a dispute between clergy. During what was an arduous journey, he became ill and his friends seeing that he was dying, gathered round him weeping, as he prayed 'Oh Lord, if I am still necessary to Thy people, I do not shrink from toil. Thy will be done.' And soon his spirit returned to his Maker with whom he longed to be.

The example set by Martin and his monks was the source of inspiration for the apostles and evangelists of Ireland and Britain who became missionaries to Europe.

The Hymn known as 'St. Patrick's Breastplate'

as translated by Mrs.C.F.Alexander

I bind unto myself today
The strong name of the Trinity,
By invocation of the same,
The Three in One and One in Three.

I bind this day to me for ever,
By power of faith, Christ's Incarnation;
His baptism in the Jordan River;
His death on cross for my salvation;
His bursting from the spicèd tomb;
His riding up the heavenly way;
His coming at the day of doom;
I bind unto myself today.

I bind unto myself the power
Of the great love of the Cherubim;
The sweet 'Well done' in judgment hour;
The service of the Seraphim,
Confessors' faith, Apostles' word,
The Patriarch's prayers, the Prophets' scrolls.
All good deeds done unto the Lord,
And purity of virgin souls.

I bind unto myself today
The virtues of the starlit heaven,
The glorious sun's life-giving ray,
The whiteness of the moon at even,
The flashing of the lightning free,
The whirling wind's tempestuous shocks,
The stable earth, the deep salt sea,
Around the old eternal rocks.

I bind unto myself today
The power of God to hold and lead,
His eye to watch, His might to stay,
His ear to hearken to my need.
The wisdom of my God to teach,
His hand to guide His shield to ward;
The word of God to give me speech,
His heavenly host to be my guard.

Against the demon snares of sin,
The vice that gives temptation force,
The natural lusts that war within,
The hostile men that mar my course;
Or few or many, far or nigh,
In every place, and in all hours
Against their fierce hostility,
I bind to me these holy powers.

Against Satan's spells and wiles,
Against false words of heresy,
Against the knowledge that defiles
Against the heart's idolatory,
Against the wizard's evil craft,
Against the death-wound and the burning
The choking wave and poisoned shaft,
Protect me, Christ, till thy returning.

Christ be with me, Christ within me,
Christ behind me, Christ before me,
Christ beside me, Christ to win me,
Christ to comfort and restore me,
Christ beneath me, Christ above me,
Christ in quiet, Christ in danger,
Christ in hearts of all that love me,
Christ in mouth of friend and stranger.

I bind unto myself the name,
The strong name of the Trinity;
By invocation of the same,
The Three in One, and One in Three,
Of whom all nature hath creation;
Eternal Father, Spirit, Word:
Praise to the Lord of my Salvation,
Salvation is of Christ the Lord.

Chapter 9

St. Patrick And Saint Nynia (Ninian)

Patrick - a Briton who became the Patron Saint of Ireland

There is still uncertainty about the date of his birth. It was probably early in the fifth century. He was born of Christian parents and had a grandfather who was a priest. There is evidence to support the belief that his home was in the Solway region, near Hadrian's Wall. A Christian Church of the fourth century has just been found in the vicinity. He had friends in Wales and some believe he was born there.

At the age of 16 he was captured by the Irish slave raiders and sold to one of the Kings in Ireland. Living conditions were extremely hard for him. These are his own words: 'After I came to Ireland... and so tended sheep every day. I often prayed in the daytime... up to a hundred prayers and at night nearly as many, and I stayed in the forest, and on the mountains before daylight, I used to be roused to prayer in the snow, and in frost and rain, and I felt no harm, nor was there any inclination to take things easily in me, because as I see now the Spirit seethed in me.'

David Adam clarifies this so well in his book of meditations on the Hymn of St Patrick, 'The Cry of the Deer'. He adds these words: 'Through constant prayer he built his living relationship with God, he knew he was not alone; and he triumphed, not in his own might, but in the power and presence of God.'

Patrick also wrote: 'And another time I also saw Him praying inside me as it seemed... so I believed, because of His indwelling Spirit which has worked in me ever since that day.' Patrick was much loved by the few who knew him. He eventually managed to escape and, with some adventures, found his way back home. He yearned to go back as a missionary. We cannot be sure whether he went straight back to Ireland, but we do know that he went to Gaul where Martin had planted Churches. It was here that he was instructed and probably ordained and where he became empowered by the Holy Spirit. He returned to Ireland with evangelistic zeal, to Derry which was the centre of Druidism.

There are many stories of his courage, of healings and miracles. With his great love and pastoral care he travelled extensively in Ireland building Churches and baptising. Although he himself was not a monk, he encouraged both men and women to consider the monastic life. Those early monasteries were religious communities of monks and nuns, some of them married, shepherded by abbots and abbesses. So began the Golden Age of Saints as Ireland sent back missionaries to Gaul and the rest of Europe. Patrick died near Wicklow where they claim his missionary journeys began.

From the hand of Patrick, we have only his 'Confessions' and his letter to Coroticus, a Pictish warlord in Dumbarton region. The so-called Hymn of St.Patrick could have been handed down by oral tradition. We have two translations: one by Kuno Meyer called 'The Deer's Cry', and the other by Mrs C.F Alexander known as 'St Patrick's Breastplate'. This is in our hymnbooks. It clearly expresses the Celtic Christians' awareness of the reality of the world of spirit, the need for protection, both spiritual and physical, their complete trust and absolute confidence in the protection of Jesus, and of the Oneness of Almighty God, Father, Son, and Holy Spirit.

It is a pity that some hymn books have left out two verses, one beginning 'Against the demon snares of sin' and the other 'Against all Satan's spells and wiles', because then the hymn only expresses the great need for protection, but gives no idea of why this is necessary! It is like arming a soldier without giving him any information about the enemy and the enemy's strategy. (full version on page 34) Do read Kuno Meyer's translation in David Adam's book, "The Cry of the Deer".

Nynia - (Now Known as Ninian)

Another Briton from the Solway was Ninian, and again there is a dispute over his date. The assumption that he was born near the end of the 4th Century led to the celebration and pilgrimages to Whithorn, but the archaeologists who exposed the site of his original Church and burial ground now have a consensus of opinion with local historians that Ninian's birth was around 430 A.D. We have no record of Ninian ever meeting Patrick although they were both born early in the Fifth Century.

There were three strong Northern tribes of Britons, the Brigantes of Northumbria, further north were the Votadini, and in the Solway region were the Novantae where Ninian's father was a prominent person in a Christian family that had probably been closely associated with Roman traders and soldiers. The Roman legions had evacuated Britain but would have left equipment and trained the Britons to resist Pictish raids and fight back, which they did. Also, the trade from the Solway to the Mediterranean had to be protected. This is what probably gave Ninian's parents the opportunity to send him to Rome for training.

It was later recorded that Ninian was ordained bishop in Rome and sent back to the Solway to establish a bishopric at Whithorn.

Ninian did not do exactly what he was sent to do because he broke his journey at Tours and stayed with the monks in the great monastic community founded by St Martin at Marmoutier. Here, like Patrick, he was fired with the same evangelistic zeal and Martin's way of launching out and planting Churches. The Spirit moved him to proceed to Whithorn with monks who were skilled masons and who built the first stone Church in this part of the world. The Church was known as Candida Casa, the shining white house. Peter Hill, the archaeologist, in his book 'Whithorn and St.Ninian' says the original builders used lime to produce a crust of calcium carbonate. People called it Martin's House. Close to many Churches dedicated to St Ninian, the name of Martin is found.

Ninian would have established a very practical community with many skills and trades alongside a seminary for training men for the priesthood and to become missionaries. He had no concern for Diocesan boundaries, as he sought to respond to the Divine Commission of Jesus to go to all the world. It is worth noting now how useful the young Britons from the aforementioned Northern tribes were going to be as missionaries to the Pictish tribes, because they were able to speak their language, something the Scots were not able to do. Ninian's missionaries went deep among the Southern Picts, many of whom became Christians, to the extent that slave raids and slave trading stopped for a long period. People filled with the Holy Spirit halted slavery among fierce pagan tribes. Why, centuries later, in a so-called Christian country, were cities allowed to be built by the slave trade?

Ninian maintained contact with the church in Rome, and supported teaching against early heresies, such as deviations from the truth of the Gospel as revealed to St. John. John was so close to Jesus, that when he was dying upon the Cross, Jesus committed his mother Mary and John into each other's care. St. John's gospel was very precious to the early Celts.

Candida Casa became a great training centre for Irish missionaries, and as the Christian faith spread among the tribes, the Picts and the Irish turned much of the energy that had gone into warfare and piracy into the development of creative skills that amounted to genius. In the early Christian centuries, their scholarship, metalwork, sculpture, book illumination, and their religious commitment made an outstanding contribution to the culture of Western Europe. The historian, Daphne Brooke, expounds this well in her book 'Wild Men and Holy Places'. Another book to read is 'St Nynia' by Professor John MacQueen.

The Growth & Vitality of the British Church

It is generally called the Celtic Church, but it could have been called the Jesus Church or the Holy Spirit Church, because they knew that they were under the control of the Three Persons of the Godhead. Each house fellowship was a living cell in the Body of Christ, and there they would break bread together. Some fellowships were hidden for a long time before it was safe to come out into the open to worship and celebrate.

There was a strongly recommended practice among those early Christians, especially in Ireland, of each person having an anamchara or soul friend; not a close companion, but another faithful Christian whom they could trust and with whom they could share confidences, weaknesses, anxieties, sinful tendencies, and who would suggest how help could be given and then check their progress at regular intervals. The value of this practice is now being rediscovered.

Chapter 10

St. Columba And St. Moluag

Early 6th Century A.D.

Comgall & Moluag, Irish Picts, and Columba, the Irish Scot

Most people know about Columba and the Isle of Iona, but few know anything about Moluag and the Isle of Lismore, whose life was entwined with Columba's. Confusion has been caused by so many legends springing up around Columba. The following is an attempt to clarify what happened.

Columba had been called Colm Cille, which means Dove of the Church, by his mother. He was a tribal prince of the Irish Gaelic speaking Scots. He became a great evangelist with a passion for gathering people into the Kingdom of God. He founded monastic communities in Kells and Derry. These were the founding days of monasteries of men and women, married and single, governed by abbots and abbesses. Brigid was perhaps the most famous of Ireland's abbesses.

Among the Picts in Ireland on the east side was Ireland's greatest Christian scholar, Comgall, called Comgall the Great, who founded monasteries and the famous religious community at Bangor. It was said of him that he kindled in the hearts of men the unquenchable fire of the love of God.

Although in rival clans, as Christians Columba was well known to Comgall the great. Moluag was a relative of Comgall and was training missionaries. He certainly would have known Columba.

One day, Columba, in his eagerness to have his own copy of the Scriptures, foolishly without permission, copied a manuscript brought back from Rome, and this caused such an uproar that it ended in tribal fighting and was recorded as the Battle of Cul Drebene 56 A.D. with at least 300 men killed. Columba was excommunicated. He became deeply penitent, was reprieved, and as a personally imposed penance, sailed away from Ireland with twelve monks to convert at least as many people as had been killed. They travelled, not in one of the oak trading ships, but in a hide-hulled currach. They would almost certainly have called at Dal Riada (Argyll region) to see their fellow Scots before reaching Hy (Iona). The date we have been given is 563 A.D.

This is where Moluag comes into the story. In that same year, Comgall the Great sent Moluag to the Isle of Lismore, which one passes when travelling from Oban to Mull. He was to build a training centre for missionaries. There is much evidence on the Isle of Lismore for anyone to see that Columba was closely associated with Moluag. They were, of course, both Irish and both zealous Christians, though in rival camps. The story they are so sure about on Lismore is that Columba and Moluag, each with twelve men in their boats, raced to see who could get the ownership of the island.

When nearly there Columba was just leading when Moluag chopped off a finger, threw it on the beach shouting, "My flesh and blood is on the island!" Columba swore at him and went to Iona. There is just a possibility that they both left Ireland at the same time.

Columba was never allowed to preach on the Isle of Lismore, except from a small island linked at low tide, where crowds gathered to hear him, though he always needed someone to interpret for the Picts. In later years, the Roman Catholic Church built a cathedral on Lismore, and on that site now is a beautiful Church used for worship by the Church of Scotland. In the Church are two very good stained glass windows of Moluag and Columba. Also located on the island is the pastoral staff of Saint Moluag. This can be seen today at the home of its hereditary keeper, the Baron of Bachuil.

41

Columba Taken to the High King of the Picts

Who took him? Again, there are many different stories, and I am sharing the one which seems most feasible. It was Comgall himself who, together with St Cainnech, arranged to meet Columba at the Isle of Lismore, and took him up the Great Glen to Inverness to see King Bruide MacMailchon. This would have been a very strategic move on the part of Comgall to encourage the king to be supportive of Pictish missionaries going deep into Pictland, even to the Western Isles. Also an encouragement to Moluag who was responsible for a missionary training centre at Rosemarkie, not far from the castle of King Bruide, thus confirming that the Christian faith was already planted in the east of Pictland with monasteries being formed there.

It is clear that the king was greatly impressed with the courage and faith of Columba, and gave his authority for Columba to live on the Isle of Iona, from where he could minister in religious affairs to his fellow Scots in the Dal Riada district of Pictland. The Picts had consistently driven the Scots back there when they had launched attacks. Bruide probably underestimated the ability and power of Columba, because it was not long before Columba appointed and crowned Aedhan (not to be confused with Aidan) as King of the Scots in Dal Riada. Also, Columba was invited back to Ireland to be crowned King of the Irish Scots, but by now he was settled on Iona, though making a few journeys to the north to preach the Gospel. The Druids and islanders became Christians and he was determined to stay and teach his monks by his example in the way of holiness. He was then becoming what his mother called him 'Dove of the Church'. It is perhaps worth noting that Columba once in prayer addressed Jesus as "My Druid" showing how the Druids were recognised as leaders and teachers.

Among his monks were those responsible for the amazing illuminations in the Book of Kells, which was eventually returned to Kells before the Viking raids. Some people wonder why those designs include such a variety of foliage and living creatures. It was because the monks had no libraries or ornate Churches in which to meditate. They sat in caves and forests very close to nature, to the tiniest insects in the grass or on the rocks, as well as to the birds and flying insects. The spiralling of plants reaching for the sun accounted for encircling concepts. Looking at the Callenish Stones on the Isle of Lewis through the seasons and all weathers shows how much those early people treasured, as well as cleverly placed for worship, what to them was unchangeable. This can teach us a lot about what was enduring to those early people, like rock, with everything else that was constantly changing.

Drawings of St.Moluag the Pict, and St.Columba the Scot, from stained glass windows in Lismore Parish Church, the Cathedral Church of St.Moluag, on the Isle of Lismore.

The Celtic monks were soaked in the Scriptures, being taught the Old Testament and the Gospels of the New Testament, especially St.John's Gospel. Without books they depended on oral teaching and young novices were given a year to learn the Psalms by heart! - in addition to the daily reading of the Scriptures, the corporate singing of Psalms and the singing of hymns of worship to God. Many would have spent hours learning to write and copy the Scriptures, in addition to the daily hymns of worship to God.

Columba died in 597 A.D. at the altar of his Church, face radiant with joy and hand outstretched in blessing. This is what he wrote just before he died:

'See that you be at peace among yourselves, my children, and love one another. Follow the example of good men of old, and God will comfort you and help you, both in this world and in the world which is to come.'

St. Martin's Cross, Isle of Iona, c800 A.D.
'This cross is one solid block of Mull granite, whose wind
resistance is reduced by having very short arms with slots
for removable wooden extensions.'
(from 'Iona' by Richard Reece)

The hillock behind the cross is Tor Abb, excavated in 1957. They
found St. Columba's cell, exactly as described by his biographer,
Adamnan, less than a hundred years after Columba's death, and now
reverently preserved and hidden beneath rocks and grass. It is good
to see the cross nearest St. Columba's cell is named after the great
founding Celtic saint, Martin of Tours.

45

The 14ᵗʰ Century Church of St. Columba at Aiguish on the
Isle of Lewis.   A great Irish saint, Catan, or Cathan, lived
in the original chapel.
St. Columba came here from Iona in A.D.563.

Chapter 11

The Age Of Saints Had Begun

With their many years of academic and practical training, the Druids who became Christians would have taught their fellowships the Scriptures, the Word of God, with thoroughness commending the learning of the Psalms by heart. The Druidical concern about morality and loyalty strengthened the family and the keeping of the Ten Commandments. The concern for morality led them on to holiness which God required of His children.

The word of God was indeed a seed, an embryo tree, planted by holy men and women in those early days. Their names are recorded everywhere in these islands: churches, towns, villages, even islands named after them. Many of these saints must have won souls for Jesus by their faith, their love, their holiness and self-control. Here are a few who were linked with people and places mentioned in these pages.

COLUMBANUS – Trained as a missionary by Abbot Comgall of Bangor in Ireland. He went to Gaul and built a Church on the site of a pagan temple. Some called him the greatest missionary among the monks who went out from Ireland.

FINTAN - Irish Abbot of Clonenagh, revered by St.Columba for his holiness.

COLMAN – trained by Columba on Iona.

FINIAN - a Briton who lived in Ireland, but came back to Whithorn to be trained as a missionary at St. Nynia's Candida Casa.

KENTIGERN - an evangelist who taught in Strathclyde, and became Bishop of Glasgow. He was called 'MUNGO' which means 'My dear one'. It should be noted that there is evidence to substantiate references to Ninian as the one who brought the Christian faith to Strathclyde.

GILDAS was born in Nothumbria. He became a great writer and commentator on the Celtic Church. He settled in a monastery in Wales, moved to near Glastonbury, visited Ireland when he was sixty-seven, and finally settled in Southern Brittany.

This lady representing "Gentle Earth" protecting God's creation in the beautiful Benedicite window of Epsom's parish Church I have named St. Melangell, because she is like that Celtic Irish princess who settled in the small Welsh valley, Pennant Melangell, where a hare ran to her for protection from hunting hounds. It is good to be reminded of her in a church dedicated to St. Martin of Tours, who was a founding father of many early Celtic saints.

Among the Welsh saints **DAVID** and **ILLTYD** are well known.   One lessor known, but getting publicity to-day is **MELANGELL**, the Irish princess who escaped from a forced marriage, crossed by coracle to Wales, wandered as far as Pennant Melangell in Powys, settled and established a small community.   Her shrine has been restored and is the oldest shrine in Wales.   The legend describes how a hare being chased by the hounds of a hunt by Prince Brochwel was miraculously protected by the virgin.   The Prince was so impressed by her godliness that he gave her and the valley his protection against hunters.

It is hard to stop without mentioning other Saints of Ireland, Cornwall, and the Isle of Man, but I only set out to describe a vision of the way God masterminded the preparation of the sowing of the seed, and the early growth of His Church.   That sowing was first done by merchants on tradeships, by Roman soldiers, by slaves and by refugees.

After 600 A.D. there were more records available of the Celtic Church and readers should know about the great **NORTHUMBRIAN SAINTS.**   **AIDAN** was taught by the monks on Iona after the death of St.Columba.   **KING OSWALD** was also taught as a youth on Iona.   **CUTHBERT** the Abbot of Lindisfarne on Holy Island, and **HILDA** the Abbess of Whitby, were famous saints of the later Celtic Church.   The arrival of **AUGUSTINE** from Rome on the Isle of Thanet heralded great changes, and the Roman Catholic Church gradually gained control over the islands where the Celtic Church had grown and blossomed.

Chapter 12

What Can We Learn From The Early Celtic Church?

The earliest converts to Christianity in these islands were people who were already fully aware of the reality of the spirit world of good and evil. Their great discovery was that God had a threefold nature. They soon had a personal relationship with Jesus, with His Father and with the Holy Spirit. They lived close to God and close to nature.

In the early Celtic Church young and old depended upon oral teaching, only monks and scholars had parchments. They listened to stories of the Greek heroes, then of Abraham, Isaac, Jacob, Joseph, Moses, the Prophets, and of Jesus. They taught from the Scriptures that Jesus Himself used. Those early missionaries, especially from Ireland, reached deep into Europe and beyond.

Their knowledge of the Scriptures encouraged them to be zealous for the saving of souls and extension of God's Kingdom. They knew the power of prayer and had the prayer support of their families and communities. They knew they had the protection of the Holy Spirit, and of angels, and they had the authority to use the Name of Jesus in a ministry of healing, and deliverance from evil spirits.

They preached the Gospel with boldness, empowered by the Holy Spirit, and witnessed miracles of healing and deliverance. We have seen this happening in Reinhard Bonnke's campaigns in Africa, proving to hundreds of thousands of people that Jesus Christ is Saviour and Lord. St. Martin, when he was bishop of Tours in the fourth century, challenges all of us today by his example of practical Christianity. He was able and eager to help people in need wherever he went, even teaching his monks how to build.

Governments of countries closed to missionaries are welcoming Christians qualified with different skills to help their people suffering through natural disasters. There are many organisations meeting this need, such as Tearfund, Interserve, Save the Children Fund, Anti-Slavery International and Aviation Fellowship. Theological seminaries alone are not sufficient. Adelaide College at Saltcoats in Ayrshire is an example of a Bible College that trains students in practical skills that are useful anywhere in the world.

Inspired by the oral teaching in the Celtic Church the Northumbria Community has arranged storytelling seminars in many places which effectively teach the word of God to young and old.

Later in the thirteenth century Francseco Bernardone, now known as St. Francis of Assisi, was earnestly praying and seeking God's guidance when he distinctly heard Jesus speaking to him. He was moved by the Holy Spirit to train men who would be willing to live in poverty, and completely surrender their lives to Jesus, sharing His lifestyle, and ready to be sent to any nation to preach the Gospel.

In a Rule of Life he exhorted his brothers to care for the poor and destitute, even to the point of identity with them. Francis had much in common with the Celtic saints but he encountered strong opposition from within his authoritarian church, turning away from the Word of God and damaged by secularization.

In our generation, in 1982, Communists took control of Ethiopia and all churches and buildings of the 5000 strong Mennonite Church were confiscated, all Christian meetings forbidden. It was not even safe to sing a hymn at home. The Church went totally underground; but it was a Cell Church, a Seed Church, like the first century each family was well-instructed in the Scriptures, the Word of God, in healing and deliverance. They understood the ministry of the Holy Spirit. At the end of ten years, in 1992, the Government was overthrown and a Church leader called all remaining members to services on a Sunday. 50,000 turned up!

Wherever members of the Body of Christ are forced to live underground in hostile pagan countries, they will grow and bear fruit if they have had sound Biblical teaching, obey the Commandments, wholly accept the words of Jesus, and live together in mutual love.

Jesus said "If you love me keep my commandments and I will pray to the Father and He will give you another Helper, that He may abide with you forever – the Spirit of truth; whom the world cannot receive, because it neither sees Him nor knows Him; but you know Him, for He dwells with you and will be in you." St. John 14: 15-17. This was known and experienced by Celtic Christians and is missing from too many lives of church members today.

Here in these islands we see the widespread breaking of God's Commandments, the worship of mammon and many false gods, lawlessness, even among children, the break-up of family life, gambling, drug addition and sexual immorality.   The call to repentance is desperately needed and, sadly, within the Church too. In addition to false teaching there is a very dangerous turning to occult practices.

If the Church fails to obey the Word of God, then He will withdraw His blessings, and the Church will come under the severe judgment of God as happened to the Children of Israel.

There are times when God moves with awesome power both to warn and to save His people. An example happened only fifty years ago. It was in 1949 on the Isle of Lewis in the Outer Hebrides. Local ministers were greatly distressed by the drunkenness and ungodly behaviour of the people. They prayed earnestly to God for His mercy and forgiveness, and for Him to do something to convince the people of sin, His righteousness and judgment.

The Holy Spirit suddenly came among the people just where they happened to be; at work in the fields, on the hills, in their boats, at their looms, as well as in their churches.   People fell on their knees and wept, crying to God for mercy.   Duncan Campbell who was brought to the island to preach the Gospel when this was taking place describes exactly what happened. His voice can be heard on a tape made only a few years later.

People in so many countries today are desperately crying out for help. From these islands and many other countries young Christians have joined the volunteers, and have gone out, and are still going out, trained by: Youth with a Mission, Youth for Christ, Operation Mobilisation, Tear Fund, Overseas Missionary Fellowship, Christian Aid, and similar missions.

They go out to meet urgent human need with the love and compassion of Jesus. A much greater number of young people here are just waiting for churches to meet them at their point of need, to listen to them, let them share their experiences, and give them a positive role in the fellowship of their church. They too will volunteer.

Crusade for World Revival, with the lead given by Selwyn Hughes, has consistently given the needed information, with a global perspective, calling intercessors to prayer and action.

My story began around 600 B.C. when the prophet Daniel, together with the People of Israel, had been taken to Babylon as slaves. The Temple in Jerusalem had been destroyed. Three hundred years earlier God had spoken to Solomon, the son of David, with promises of blessings and warnings of punishment for sin. Solomon became the richest and wisest of kings with further promises of blessings, yet he flagrantly disobeyed God and failed to keep His commandments. God knew what was going to happen when He spoke to Solomon. It seems appropriate that we should end with God's words and take them to our hearts today.

"If My people who are called by My Name, humble themselves and pray, and seek My face, and turn from their wicked ways, then I will hear them from heaven, will forgive their sin, and will heal their land."

(2 Chronicles 7 : v 14)

Helpful Books

PICTS
by Anna Ritchie
Historic Buildings and Monuments.
H.M.S.O. Edinburgh.

PICTISH TRAIL
by Anthony Jackson.
The Orkney Press.

NEW LIGHT ON THE CALLENISH STONES.
G.&M.Ponting.
Essprint Ltd., Stornoway.

THE MEANING OF SCOTLAND'S SYMBOL STONES.
Edward Peterson
P.C.D. Ruthven Books

STONE AGE ALPHA
Edward Peterson
P.C.D. Ruthven Books

THE CRY OF THE DEER
David Adam
Triangle. B.P.C.Paperbacks Ltd.

MARTIN OF TOURS
Christopher Donaldson
Canterbury Press

WILD MEN & HOLY PLACES
Daphne Brooke
Canongate Press

ST.NYNIA
John MacQueen
Polygon Edinburgh

THE FURY OF THE NORTHMEN
John Marsden
Kyle Kathie Limited.

SEA-ROAD OF THE SAINTS
John Marsden
Floris Books

WHAT IS CELTIC CHRISTIANITY?
Elizabeth Culling
Grove Series on Spirituality No.45

WHITHORN and ST.NINIAN
Peter Hill
A complete record of the Excavations

CELT, DRUID & CULDEE
Isabel Hill Elder
Covenant Books

SAINTS, SEAWAYS and SETTLEMENTS
E.G.Bowen
Cardiff University of Wales Press